20 best
pizza recipes

D1569025

Houghton Mifflin Harcourt
Boston • New York • 2013

For information about permission to reproduce selections from this book, write to Permissions, Houghton Mifflin Harcourt Publishing Company, 215 Park Avenue South, New York, New York 10003.

www.hmhco.com

Cover photo: Fresh Mozzarella and Tomato Pizza (page 6)

General Mills
Food Content and Relationship Marketing Director: Geoff Johnson
Food Content Marketing Manager: Susan Klobuchar
Senior Editor: Grace Wells
Kitchen Manager: Ann Stuart
Recipe Development and Testing: Betty Crocker Kitchens
Photography: General Mills Photography Studios and Image Library

Houghton Mifflin Harcourt
Publisher: Natalie Chapman
Editorial Director: Cindy Kitchel
Executive Editor: Anne Ficklen
Associate Editor: Heather Dabah
Managing Editor: Rebecca Springer
Production Editor: Kristi Hart
Cover Design: Chrissy Kurpeski
Book Design: Tai Blanche

ISBN 978-0-544-31483-2
Printed in the United States of America

The Betty Crocker Kitchens seal guarantees success in your kitchen. Every recipe has been tested in America's Most Trusted Kitchens™ to meet our high standards of reliability, easy preparation and great taste.

FIND MORE GREAT IDEAS AT
Betty Crocker.com

Dear Friends,

This new collection of colorful mini books has been put together with you in mind because we know that you love great recipes and enjoy cooking and baking but have a busy lifestyle. So every little book in the series contains just 20 recipes for you to treasure and enjoy. Plus, each book is a single subject designed in a bite-size format just for you—it's easy to use and is filled with favorite recipes from the Betty Crocker Kitchens!

All of the books are conveniently divided into short chapters so you can quickly find what you're looking for, and the beautiful photos throughout are sure to entice you into making the delicious recipes. In the series, you'll discover a fabulous array of recipes to spark your interest—from cookies, cupcakes and birthday cakes to party ideas for a variety of occasions. There's grilled foods, potluck favorites and even gluten-free recipes too.

You'll love the variety in these mini books—so pick one or choose them all for your cooking pleasure.

Enjoy and happy cooking!

Sincerely,

Betty Crocker

contents

Fresh Mozzarella and Tomato Pizza

Prep Time: 35 Minutes • **Start to Finish:** 3 Hours 15 Minutes • Makes 8 servings

1 In large bowl, dissolve yeast in warm water. Stir in half of the flour, the salt, sugar and 1 teaspoon oil. Stir in enough of the remaining flour to make dough easy to handle. Place dough on lightly floured surface. Knead about 10 minutes or until smooth and springy. Grease large bowl with shortening. Place dough in bowl, turning dough to grease all sides. Cover; let rise in warm place 20 minutes. Gently push fist into dough to deflate. Cover; refrigerate at least 2 hours but no longer than 48 hours. (If dough should double in size during refrigeration, gently push fist into dough to deflate.)

2 Move oven rack to lowest position. Heat oven to 425°F. Grease cookie sheet or 12-inch pizza pan with oil. Sprinkle with cornmeal. Using floured fingers, pat dough into 12-inch round on cookie sheet or pat in pizza pan. Press dough from center to edge so edge is slightly thicker than center.

3 Cut cheese into ¼-inch slices. Place cheese on dough to within ½ inch of edge. Arrange tomatoes on cheese. Sprinkle with salt, pepper, 2 tablespoons of the basil, the oregano and capers. Drizzle with 1 tablespoon oil.

4 Bake about 20 minutes or until crust is golden brown and cheese is melted. Sprinkle with remaining 2 tablespoons basil.

1 Slice: Calories 140; Total Fat 5g (Saturated Fat 2g, Trans Fat 0g); Cholesterol 10mg; Sodium 300mg; Total Carbohydrate 17g (Dietary Fiber 1g); Protein 6g **Exchanges:** 1 Starch, 1 Fat **Carbohydrate Choices:** 1

Shredded Mozzarella and Tomato Pizza: Substitute 2 cups shredded mozzarella cheese (8 oz) for the fresh mozzarella. Sprinkle 1 cup of the cheese over dough. Add remaining ingredients as directed—except sprinkle with remaining 1 cup cheese before drizzling with oil.

Tip Fresh mozzarella is very different from the familiar blocks of mozzarella or shredded mozzarella. The fresh version is usually made with whole milk, is white colored and has a delicate, sweet, milky flavor and much softer texture. Some cheese shops, delis and large supermarkets may carry an Italian import called "buffalo mozzarella," which is made with water buffalo milk or a combination of cow's and water buffalo milk. Fresh mozzarella is packed in water or whey and is often formed into balls or slices.

Crust

1 package regular active or fast-acting dry yeast (2¼ teaspoons)

½ cup warm water (105°F to 115°F)

1¼ to 1½ cups Gold Medal® all-purpose flour

½ teaspoon salt

½ teaspoon sugar

1 teaspoon olive oil

Topping

4 oz fresh mozzarella cheese, well drained

2 plum (Roma) tomatoes, thinly sliced

¼ teaspoon salt

Freshly ground pepper to taste

¼ cup thin strips fresh basil leaves

1 tablespoon chopped fresh oregano leaves

1 tablespoon small capers, if desired

1 tablespoon olive oil

Tomato-Basil Pizza

Prep Time: 15 Minutes • **Start to Finish:** 35 Minutes • Makes 8 servings

2¼ cups Original Bisquick®
  mix

¼ to ⅓ cup cornmeal

⅔ cup milk

1 jar (10 oz) basil pesto

1 plum (Roma) tomato, thinly
  sliced

2 cups shredded mozzarella
  cheese (8 oz)

½ cup shredded Parmesan
  cheese

¼ cup thinly sliced fresh basil
  leaves

1 tablespoon olive oil

1 Heat oven to 450°F. Spray large cookie sheet with cooking spray.

2 In large bowl, stir Bisquick mix, ¼ cup cornmeal, and milk until soft dough forms.

3 Press dough into 13 x 9-inch rectangle on cookie sheet, sprinkling with additional cornmeal as needed to prevent sticking. Pierce dough at 1-inch intervals with a fork. Bake 8 minutes, or until just beginning to brown.

4 Spread pesto over crust. Top with tomato and cheeses. Bake 8 to 10 minutes longer, or until cheese is melted. Sprinkle with basil and olive oil.

1 Serving: Calories 480; Total Fat 33g (Saturated Fat 10g, Trans Fat 1.5g); Cholesterol 30mg; Sodium 980mg; Total Carbohydrate 31g (Dietary Fiber 2g); Protein 17g **Exchanges:** 2 Starch, 1½ High-Fat Meat, 4 Fat **Carbohydrate Choices:** 2

Tip Go greener! In addition to chopped fresh basil, sprinkle ¼ cup thinly sliced arugula over the baked pizza.

Caribbean Black Bean Pizza

Prep Time: 15 Minutes • **Start to Finish:** 30 Minutes • Makes 6 servings

1 can (13.8 oz) refrigerated classic pizza crust or 1 can (11 oz) refrigerated thin pizza crust

1 can (8 oz) no-salt-added tomato sauce

2 cans (15 oz each) black beans, drained, rinsed

1 can (8 oz) pineapple tidbits in juice, well drained

½ fresh lime or 4 teaspoons lime juice

2 tablespoons chopped fresh cilantro

1½ cups shredded mozzarella cheese (6 oz)

1 If using classic crust: Heat oven to 425°F. Spray or grease 15 x 10 x 1-inch pan. Unroll dough in pan. Starting at center, press out dough to edge of pan. If using thin crust: Heat oven to 400°F. Spray or grease 15 x 10-inch or larger dark or nonstick cookie sheet. Unroll dough on cookie sheet. Starting at center, press dough into 15 x 10-inch rectangle.

2 Spread tomato sauce evenly over crust. Top with beans and pineapple. Squeeze lime juice over toppings. Top with cilantro and cheese.

3 Bake classic crust 12 to 15 minutes, thin crust 11 to 14 minutes, or until bottom of crust is deep golden brown.

1 Serving: Calories 400; Total Fat 8g (Saturated Fat 4.5g, Trans Fat 0g); Cholesterol 15mg; Sodium 1090mg; Total Carbohydrate 61g (Dietary Fiber 7g); Protein 20g **Exchanges:** 2½ Starch, 1½ Other Carbohydrate, 1½ Lean Meat, ½ Fat **Carbohydrate Choices:** 4

Tip If desired, 1 cup (4 ounces) chopped 97% fat-free smoked turkey breast can be substituted for 1 can of the beans.

Tuscan Broccoli Pizza

Prep Time: 20 Minutes • **Start to Finish:** 30 Minutes • Makes 8 servings

1 bag (11.8 oz) frozen Tuscan seasoned broccoli

1 can (13.8 oz) refrigerated artisan pizza crust with whole grain

1 tablespoon olive oil

1 clove garlic, finely chopped

1 cup sliced fresh mushrooms (3 oz)

½ cup sliced sun-dried tomatoes in oil

1½ cups shredded Italian cheese blend (6 oz)

½ teaspoon crushed red pepper flakes, if desired

1 Heat oven to 400°F. Grease large dark cookie sheet with shortening or cooking spray.

2 Cook broccoli as directed on bag; cool 10 minutes.

3 Meanwhile, unroll dough on cookie sheet; starting at center, press into 15 x 12-inch rectangle. Bake about 8 minutes or until light golden brown.

4 In small bowl, mix oil and garlic. Brush on pizza crust. Top with mushrooms, broccoli, tomatoes, cheese and pepper flakes.

5 Bake 8 to 10 minutes or until crust is deep golden brown and cheese is melted.

1 Serving: Calories 280; Total Fat 14g (Saturated Fat 4.5g, Trans Fat 0g); Cholesterol 20mg; Sodium 600mg; Total Carbohydrate 28g (Dietary Fiber 3g); Protein 11g **Exchanges:** 1½ Starch, 1 Vegetable, ½ Medium-Fat Meat, 2 Fat **Carbohydrate Choices:** 2

Mediterranean Pizza

Prep Time: 20 Minutes • **Start to Finish:** 35 Minutes • Makes 6 servings

Crust

2 tablespoons cornmeal

2½ cups Original Bisquick mix

1 package fast-acting dry yeast (2¼ teaspoons)

½ cup plus 3 tablespoons warm water (105°F to 115°F)

Topping

½ cup basil pesto

½ cup sun-dried tomatoes in oil, drained, cut into ½-inch pieces

1 can (14 oz) artichoke hearts, drained, chopped

1 cup shredded mozzarella cheese (4 oz)

1 package (4 oz) crumbled feta cheese (1 cup)

1 Heat oven to 425°F. Lightly grease 15 x 10 x 1-inch pan with shortening or cooking spray. Sprinkle with cornmeal, tapping off any excess.

2 In large bowl, stir Bisquick mix and yeast. Add water; stir until dough leaves side of bowl. On surface sprinkled with additional Bisquick mix, lightly knead dough 1 minute. Roll out to 15 x 10-inch rectangle. Place dough in pan; crimp edges, forming a rim.

3 Spread pesto over dough. Sprinkle tomatoes, artichokes, mozzarella cheese and feta cheese evenly over top.

4 Bake 12 to 15 minutes or until cheese is melted and crust is golden brown.

1 Serving: Calories 500; Total Fat 27g (Saturated Fat 10g, Trans Fat 2.5g); Cholesterol 35mg; Sodium 1270mg; Total Carbohydrate 48g (Dietary Fiber 8g); Protein 15g **Exchanges:** 3 Starch, 1 Medium-Fat Meat, 4 Fat **Carbohydrate Choices:** 3

Tip If you're an olive fan, top the pizza with sliced ripe olives or Greek olives to continue the Mediterranean theme.

Roasted Vegetable Pizza

Prep Time: 25 Minutes • **Start to Finish:** 50 Minutes • Makes 6 servings

1 cup sliced fresh mushrooms

1 medium yellow or red bell
pepper, cut into 1-inch pieces

1 medium onion, cut into thin
wedges

3 tablespoons olive oil

¾ teaspoon coarse (kosher or
sea) salt

2 cups Gold Medal all-purpose
flour

1 tablespoon sugar

1¼ teaspoons regular active
dry yeast

¾ cup warm water

2 tablespoons chopped fresh
basil

2 cans (14.5 oz each)
fire-roasted diced tomatoes,
drained

1 package (4 oz) crumbled
goat cheese

1 Heat oven to 450°F. In ungreased 15 x 10 x 1-inch pan,
toss mushrooms, bell pepper and onion with 1 tablespoon
of the oil. Sprinkle with ¼ teaspoon of the salt; toss to mix.
Spread evenly in pan. Bake 12 to 16 minutes, stirring once,
until vegetables are tender.

2 Meanwhile, in medium bowl, stir 1 cup of the flour, the
sugar, yeast, remaining ½ teaspoon salt, the warm water
and 1 tablespoon of the remaining oil. Beat with electric
mixer on low speed 30 seconds. Beat on high speed 1
minute. Stir in remaining 1 cup flour and the basil to form
a soft dough.

3 On lightly floured surface, knead dough about 5
minutes or until smooth and elastic. Cover; let rest 10
minutes.

4 Spray large cookie sheet with cooking spray. On cookie
sheet, press dough into 14 x 10-inch rectangle; prick with
fork. Bake 12 to 14 minutes or until light golden brown.

5 Brush crust with remaining 1 tablespoon oil. Spread
roasted vegetable mixture and tomatoes evenly over
crust; sprinkle with cheese. Bake 6 to 8 minutes longer or
until vegetables are warm and cheese is softened.

1 Serving: Calories 320; Total Fat 13g (Saturated Fat 5g, Trans Fat 0g); Cholesterol 15mg; Sodium 510mg; Total Carbohydrate 42g (Dietary Fiber 3g); Protein
10g **Exchanges:** 1½ Starch, 1 Other Carbohydrate, 1 Vegetable, ½ High-Fat
Meat, 1½ Fat **Carbohydrate Choices:** 3

Tip Serve with a simple green salad of mixed baby
greens tossed with your favorite vinaigrette and some
toasted pine nuts.

Garden-Fresh Alfredo Pizza

Prep Time: 15 Minutes • **Start to Finish:** 30 Minutes • Makes 8 servings

1 package (14 oz) prebaked
original Italian pizza crust
(11 inch)

½ cup refrigerated Alfredo
pasta sauce (from 10-oz
container)

1 plum (Roma) tomato,
seeded, coarsely chopped

½ cup chopped yellow bell
pepper

1 small zucchini, sliced (1 cup)

1 jar (4.5 oz) sliced
mushrooms, drained

¼ cup chopped red onion

¼ cup chopped fresh basil

1½ cups shredded Italian
cheese blend (6 oz)

1 Heat oven to 450°F. Place crust on 12-inch pizza pan or large cookie sheet. Spread Alfredo sauce over crust. Top with remaining ingredients.

2 Bake 10 to 14 minutes or until cheese is melted and crust is golden brown.

1 Serving: Calories 280; Total Fat 13g (Saturated Fat 7g, Trans Fat 0g); Cholesterol 35mg; Sodium 470mg; Total Carbohydrate 31g (Dietary Fiber 2g); Protein 10g **Exchanges:** 1½ Starch, 1 Vegetable, ½ Medium-Fat Meat, 2 Fat **Carbohydrate Choices:** 2

Tip To quickly seed a tomato, cut it in half lengthwise and use a small spoon to scrape out the seeds from each half.

Greek Chicken Pizza

Prep Time: 15 Minutes • **Start to Finish:** 30 Minutes • Makes 4 servings

1 can (13.8 oz) refrigerated classic pizza crust

1 can (8 oz) pizza sauce

1½ cups shredded mozzarella cheese (6 oz)

2 cups cubed cooked chicken

½ cup thinly sliced red onion

½ cup crumbled feta cheese (2 oz)

¼ cup chopped kalamata olives

1 tablespoon chopped fresh or 1 teaspoon dried oregano leaves

1 Heat oven to 425°F. Spray large cookie sheet with cooking spray. Unroll dough on cookie sheet; starting at center, press dough into 13 x 9-inch rectangle.

2 Spread pizza sauce over dough to within ½ inch of edges. Top with remaining ingredients.

3 Bake 12 to 15 minutes or until crust is golden brown and cheese is melted.

1 Serving: Calories 610; Total Fat 24g (Saturated Fat 12g, Trans Fat 0.5g); Cholesterol 105mg; Sodium 1410mg; Total Carbohydrate 56g (Dietary Fiber 3g); Protein 44g **Exchanges:** 2½ Starch, 1 Other Carbohydrate, ½ Vegetable, 5 Lean Meat, 1½ Fat **Carbohydrate Choices:** 4

Tip For a little flavor twist, use tomato-basil feta cheese or another favorite flavor in place of the plain feta.

Mexican Chicken Pizza with Cornmeal Crust

Prep Time: 20 Minutes • **Start to Finish:** 40 Minutes • Makes 6 servings

1½ cups Gold Medal all-purpose flour

1 tablespoon sugar

1¼ teaspoons regular active dry yeast

¼ teaspoon coarse (kosher or sea) salt

¾ cup warm water

1 tablespoon olive oil

⅓ cup yellow cornmeal

Additional cornmeal

2 cups shredded Mexican cheese blend (8 oz)

1½ cups shredded cooked chicken

1 can (14.5 oz) fire-roasted diced tomatoes or plain diced tomatoes, drained

½ medium yellow bell pepper, chopped (½ cup)

¼ cup sliced green onions (4 medium)

¼ cup chopped fresh cilantro

1 Heat oven to 450°F. In medium bowl, mix ¾ cup of the flour, the sugar, yeast and salt. Stir in warm water and oil. Beat with electric mixer on low speed 30 seconds. Beat on high speed 1 minute. Stir in ⅓ cup cornmeal and remaining ¾ cup flour to make a soft dough.

2 On lightly floured surface, knead dough until smooth and elastic, about 5 minutes. Cover; let rest 10 minutes.

3 Spray large cookie sheet with cooking spray; sprinkle with additional cornmeal. On cookie sheet, press dough into 14 x 10-inch rectangle; prick with fork. Bake 8 to 10 minutes or until edges just begin to turn brown.

4 Sprinkle with 1 cup of the cheese blend. Top with chicken, tomatoes and bell pepper. Sprinkle with remaining 1 cup cheese. Bake 6 to 8 minutes longer or until cheese is melted and edges are golden brown. Sprinkle with onions and cilantro.

1 Serving: Calories 390; Total Fat 17g (Saturated Fat 8g, Trans Fat 0g); Cholesterol 65mg; Sodium 430mg; Total Carbohydrate 36g (Dietary Fiber 2g); Protein 23g **Exchanges:** 1½ Starch, ½ Other Carbohydrate, 1 Vegetable, 2½ Medium-Fat Meat, 1 Fat **Carbohydrate Choices:** 2½

Tip Short on time? Purchase a rotisserie chicken and use it to make this pizza.

Grilled White Chicken Pizza with Caramelized Sweet Onions

Prep Time: 30 Minutes • **Start to Finish:** 40 Minutes • Makes 4 servings

2 tablespoons butter or margarine

3 cups halved thinly sliced sweet onions

1 teaspoon sugar

1 teaspoon fresh thyme leaves

2 oz cream cheese

1 package (14 oz) prebaked original Italian pizza crust (12 inch)

⅓ cup refrigerated Alfredo pasta sauce (from 10-oz container)

1 cup shredded cooked chicken

1 In 10-inch skillet, melt butter over medium heat. Cook onions and sugar in butter 20 to 25 minutes, stirring frequently, until deep golden brown and caramelized; stir in thyme.

2 Heat gas or charcoal grill. Spread cream cheese evenly over pizza crust. Top with Alfredo sauce, shredded chicken and onions. Place on grill over medium-low heat. Cover grill; cook 8 to 10 minutes or until hot.

1 Serving: Calories 570; Total Fat 28g (Saturated Fat 13g, Trans Fat 1g); Cholesterol 80mg; Sodium 770mg; Total Carbohydrate 59g (Dietary Fiber 4g); Protein 19g **Exchanges:** 4 Starch, 1 Lean Meat, 4 Fat **Carbohydrate Choices:** 4

Tip For extra flavor, substitute garlic-and-herbs spreadable cheese for the cream cheese.

Parmesan-Crusted Chicken Alfredo Pizza

Prep Time: 15 Minutes • **Start to Finish:** 30 Minutes • Makes 6 servings

1 can (13.8 oz) refrigerated classic pizza crust

2 tablespoons butter, softened

½ cup shredded Parmesan cheese (2 oz)

¾ cup Alfredo pasta sauce (from 15-oz jar)

2 cups chopped cooked chicken

1½ cups packed fresh spinach leaves

1 cup shredded Italian cheese blend or shredded mozzarella cheese (4 oz)

1 Heat oven to 400°F. Grease large dark or nonstick cookie sheet with shortening or cooking spray. Unroll dough on cookie sheet. Starting at center, press dough into 15 x 10-inch rectangle.

2 Spread butter over dough. Sprinkle Parmesan cheese evenly over butter. Bake 7 minutes; remove from oven.

3 Meanwhile, in medium bowl, mix Alfredo sauce and chicken; spoon evenly over partially baked crust. Top with spinach and cheese.

4 Bake 5 to 7 minutes longer or until cheese is melted and crust is golden brown.

1 Serving: Calories 480; Total Fat 26g (Saturated Fat 14g, Trans Fat 1g); Cholesterol 105mg; Sodium 1150mg; Total Carbohydrate 34g (Dietary Fiber 1g); Protein 28g **Exchanges:** 2½ Starch, 2 Lean Meat, 1 High-Fat Meat, 2 Fat **Carbohydrate Choices:** 2

Tip Grated Parmesan cheese can be substituted for the shredded, but it will not be as visible on the crust as the shredded.

Spicy Grilled Thai Pizza

Prep Time: 25 Minutes • **Start to Finish:** 25 Minutes • Makes 4 servings

1 package (10 oz) prebaked
Italian pizza crusts (8 inch)

¼ cup peanut sauce

1½ cups chopped cooked
chicken breast

½ cup shredded carrot

2 medium green onions,
chopped (2 tablespoons)

2 tablespoons coarsely
chopped peanuts, if desired

⅔ cup finely shredded
mozzarella cheese

2 tablespoons chopped fresh
cilantro

1 Heat gas or charcoal grill. Spread each pizza crust with
2 tablespoons of the peanut sauce. Top each pizza with
chicken, carrot, onions and peanuts. Sprinkle with cheese.

2 Place sheet of heavy-duty foil on grill; place pizzas on
foil over medium heat. Cover grill; cook 8 to 10 minutes,
moving pizzas around grill every 2 minutes to prevent
bottoms from burning, until cheese is melted. Sprinkle
with cilantro.

1 Serving: Calories 390; Total Fat 14g (Saturated Fat 6g, Trans Fat 0g);
Cholesterol 60mg; Sodium 550mg; Total Carbohydrate 35g (Dietary Fiber
2g); Protein 30g **Exchanges:** 2 Starch, 3½ Lean Meat, ½ Fat **Carbohydrate
Choices:** 2

BBQ Chicken Pizza: Substitute barbecue sauce for the
peanut sauce. Omit the carrot and chopped peanuts. Use
Cheddar cheese instead of the mozzarella.

Chicken Alfredo Pizza: Substitute Alfredo sauce for the
peanut sauce. Omit the peanuts. Use Gruyere cheese
instead of the mozzarella.

Tip These pizzas can easily be made in the oven. Heat
oven to 450°F. Bake on an ungreased cookie sheet 8 to 10
minutes.

Buffalo Chicken–Beer Bread Pizza

Prep Time: 35 Minutes • **Start to Finish:** 1 Hour 15 Minutes • Makes 6 servings

1 Heat oven to 450°F. In medium bowl, mix 1 cup of the flour, the sugar, yeast, baking powder and salt. Stir in ¾ cup beer and the oil. Beat with electric mixer on low speed 30 seconds, then on High speed 1 minute. Stir in remaining 1 cup flour to make a soft dough.

2 On lightly floured surface, knead dough until smooth and elastic, about 5 minutes. Cover; let rest 30 minutes.

3 Spray large cookie sheet with cooking spray. On cookie sheet, press dough into 14 x 10-inch rectangle; prick with fork. Bake about 10 minutes or until edges just begin to turn brown.

4 While crust is baking, in medium bowl, mix wing sauce, 2 tablespoons beer and the melted butter. Add chicken; toss to coat.

5 Remove crust from oven. In small bowl, mix shredded mozzarella and provolone cheeses. Sprinkle crust with 1 cup of the cheese mixture. Top with chicken mixture; sprinkle with remaining 1 cup cheese mixture and the blue cheese. Return to oven; bake 8 to 10 minutes longer or until cheese is melted and crust is deep golden brown. Sprinkle with green onions.

Crust

2 cups Gold Medal all-purpose flour

1 tablespoon sugar

1 package regular active dry yeast (2¼ teaspoons)

1 teaspoon baking powder

1 teaspoon coarse (kosher or sea) salt

¾ cup lager beer, such as a Boston lager, warmed to 105°F

2 tablespoons olive oil

Topping

¼ cup Buffalo wing sauce

2 tablespoons lager beer, such as a Boston lager

1 tablespoon butter, melted

1½ cups chopped cooked chicken

1 cup shredded mozzarella cheese (4 oz)

1 cup shredded provolone cheese (4 oz)

⅓ cup crumbled blue cheese

2 tablespoons sliced green onions (2 medium)

1 Serving: Calories 440; Total Fat 20g (Saturated Fat 9g, Trans Fat 0g); Cholesterol 65mg; Sodium 1210mg; Total Carbohydrate 37g (Dietary Fiber 1g); Protein 26g **Exchanges:** 2½ Starch, ½ Very Lean Meat, 1 Lean Meat, 1 High-Fat Meat, 1½ Fat **Carbohydrate Choices:** 2½

Tip Add ¼ cup chopped celery to the top of the pizza for an additional freshness.

Gluten-Free Pizza

Prep Time: 10 Minutes • **Start to Finish:** 40 Minutes • Makes 6 servings

1⅓ cups Bisquick® Gluten Free mix

½ teaspoon Italian seasoning or dried basil

½ cup water

⅓ cup oil

2 eggs, beaten

1 can (8 oz) pizza sauce

1 cup bite-size pieces favorite meat or vegetables

1½ cups shredded mozzarella cheese (6 oz)

1 Heat oven to 425°F. Grease 12-inch pizza pan. Stir Bisquick mix, Italian seasoning, water, oil and eggs until well combined. Spread in pan.

2 Bake 15 minutes (crust will appear cracked).

3 Spread pizza sauce over crust; top with meat and cheese.

4 Bake 10 to 15 minutes longer or until cheese is melted.

1 Serving: Calories 230; Total Fat 14g (Saturated Fat 2.5g, Trans Fat 0g); Cholesterol 70mg; Sodium 320mg; Total Carbohydrate 23g (Dietary Fiber 0g); Protein 3g **Exchanges:** 1½ Starch, 2½ Fat **Carbohydrate Choices:** 1½

Tip Cooking gluten free? Always read labels to make sure each recipe ingredient is gluten free. Products and ingredient sources can change.

Salsa Pizza with Cheese Crust

Prep Time: 15 Minutes • **Start to Finish:** 45 Minutes • Makes 8 servings

1 lb lean (at least 80%)
  ground beef

1¼ cups chunky-style salsa

2 cups Original Bisquick mix

¼ cup mild salsa-flavor or
  jalapeño-flavor process
  cheese spread

¼ cup hot water

4 medium green onions, sliced
  (½ cup)

1 cup shredded Colby–
  Monterey Jack cheese (4 oz)

1 Heat oven to 375°F. Grease large cookie sheet.

2 In 10-inch skillet, cook beef over medium heat, stirring occasionally, until brown; drain. Stir in salsa; remove from heat.

3 In medium bowl, stir Bisquick mix, cheese spread and hot water until soft dough forms. On surface sprinkled with additional Bisquick mix, roll dough in Bisquick mix to coat. Shape into ball; knead 5 times. Press dough into 14-inch round; place on cookie sheet.

4 Spread beef mixture over crust to within 2 inches of edge. Sprinkle with onions. Fold edge over beef mixture. Sprinkle with cheese.

5 Bake 25 to 28 minutes or until crust is golden brown and cheese is melted.

1 Serving: Calories 300; Total Fat 18g (Saturated Fat 8g, Trans Fat 7g); Cholesterol 50mg; Sodium 700mg; Total Carbohydrate 21g (Dietary Fiber 1g); Protein 17g **Exchanges:** 1 Starch, 1 Vegetable, 2 High-Fat Meat **Carbohydrate Choices:**

Tip For a spicier crust, use jalapeño-flavor process cheese. Also, try garnishing the pizza with chopped tomato and shredded lettuce.

Caprese Pizza with Crispy Pancetta

Prep Time: 30 Minutes • **Start to Finish:** 1 Hour • Makes 8 servings

1 tablespoon yellow cornmeal

1½ cups Original Bisquick mix

1½ teaspoons Italian seasoning

⅓ cup hot water

1 tablespoon olive oil

⅓ cup refrigerated basil pesto

3 medium tomatoes, cut into ¼-inch slices

8 oz fresh mozzarella cheese, cut into ¼-inch slices, or 1½ cups shredded mozzarella cheese (6 oz)

2 oz sliced pancetta or bacon, crisply cooked, crumbled

¼ cup fresh basil leaves, torn

3 tablespoons balsamic vinegar

1 Heat oven to 350°F. Spray 12-inch pizza pan with cooking spray; sprinkle with cornmeal.

2 In medium bowl, stir Bisquick mix, Italian seasoning, hot water and oil until soft dough forms. On surface lightly sprinkled with additional Bisquick mix; knead dough until smooth. Press dough in pan. Bake 10 minutes.

3 Spread pesto over warm crust. Arrange tomatoes and mozzarella in circles on top of pesto, overlapping tomato and cheese slices. Bake 15 to 20 minutes longer or until crust is golden brown and cheese is melted. Sprinkle with pancetta and basil. Drizzle with balsamic vinegar.

1 Serving: Calories 300; Total Fat 19g (Saturated Fat 7g, Trans Fat 0g); Cholesterol 0mg; Sodium 700mg; Total Carbohydrate 20g (Dietary Fiber 1g); Protein 13g **Exchanges:** 1 Starch, ½ Low-Fat Milk, ½ Lean Meat, 2½ Fat **Carbohydrate Choices:** 1

Tip Sprinkling the pizza pan with cornmeal after spraying adds to the crispness of the crust.

Loaded Baked Potato Pizza

Prep Time: 10 Minutes • **Start to Finish:** 30 Minutes • Makes 6 servings

1 package (14 oz) prebaked original Italian pizza crust (12 inch)

½ cup chive-and-onion sour cream potato topper (from 12-oz container)

1 cup refrigerated homestyle potato slices (from 20-oz bag)

1 tablespoon olive or vegetable oil

¼ teaspoon pepper

8 slices bacon, crisply cooked, coarsely chopped

1 small tomato, seeded, chopped (½ cup)

1 cup shredded Cheddar cheese (4 oz)

2 tablespoons chopped fresh chives

1 Heat oven to 400°F. Place pizza crust on ungreased cookie sheet. Spread potato topper over crust to within ½ inch of edge.

2 In medium bowl, mix potatoes, oil and pepper; spoon over sour cream topper. Sprinkle with bacon, tomato, cheese and chives.

3 Bake 18 to 20 minutes or until potatoes are thoroughly heated and cheese is melted. If desired, drizzle additional potato topper over pizza.

1 Serving: Calories 410; Total Fat 21g (Saturated Fat 9g, Trans Fat 0g); Cholesterol 35mg; Sodium 830mg; Total Carbohydrate 38g (Dietary Fiber 1g); Protein 16g **Exchanges:** 2½ Starch, 1 Medium-Fat Meat, 3 Fat **Carbohydrate Choices:** 2½

Tip Change up the toppings with what you have on hand, such as adding cooked broccoli florets and sprinkling with chopped green onions instead of chives. Use chopped cooked ham instead of the bacon, if you prefer.

Ham and Gorgonzola Pizza

Prep Time: 20 Minutes • **Start to Finish:** 1 Hour • Makes 6 servings

Crust

2½ to 3 cups Gold Medal all-purpose flour

1 tablespoon sugar

1 teaspoon salt

1 package regular active or fast-acting dry yeast (2¼ teaspoons)

3 tablespoons olive or vegetable oil

1 cup very warm water (120°F to 130°F)

Topping

1 teaspoon olive oil

⅓ cup refrigerated Alfredo sauce

1 cup cubed cooked ham

½ cup crumbled Gorgonzola or blue cheese (2 oz)

4 medium green onions, sliced (¼ cup)

1 cup shredded mozzarella cheese (4 oz)

½ teaspoon dried oregano leaves

1 In large bowl, mix 1 cup of the flour, the sugar, salt and yeast. Add 3 tablespoons oil and the warm water; mix well. Stir in enough remaining flour until dough is soft and leaves side of bowl. On lightly floured surface, knead dough 4 to 5 minutes or until smooth and springy. Cover loosely with plastic wrap; let rest 10 minutes.

2 Heat oven to 425°F. Spray large cookie sheet or 12-inch pizza pan with cooking spray.

3 Divide dough in half.* Press half of dough into 12-inch round on cookie sheet. Brush dough with 1 teaspoon oil. Bake 10 to 12 minutes or until crust is golden brown.

4 Spread Alfredo sauce over crust. Sprinkle with ham, Gorgonzola cheese, onions, mozzarella cheese and oregano. Bake 9 to 11 minutes longer or until cheese is melted.

You can make 2 pizzas right away if you're serving a larger group. Just press and bake the other half of the dough on a second pizza pan and double the toppings. Or prebake the second crust, only through step 3, then wrap it tightly in plastic wrap and freeze. Unwrap and thaw before topping and baking as directed in step 4.

1 Serving: Calories 460; Total Fat 22g (Saturated Fat 9g, Trans Fat 0g); Cholesterol 45mg; Sodium 1060mg; Total Carbohydrate 45g (Dietary Fiber 2g); Protein 20g **Exchanges:** 3 Starch, 1 Medium-Fat Meat, 3 Fat **Carbohydrate Choices:** 3

Grilled Kielbasa, Caramelized Onion and Basil Pizzas

Prep Time: 45 Minutes • **Start to Finish:** 45 Minutes • Makes 4 individual pizzas

1 tablespoon olive or
vegetable oil

1 small red onion, thinly sliced
(about ¾ cup)

Olive oil cooking spray

1 can (13.8 oz) refrigerated
classic pizza crust

¾ cup pizza sauce

1 cup (about 4 oz) thinly sliced
cooked kielbasa sausage
(from 16-oz package)

1 cup shredded mozzarella
cheese (4 oz)

½ cup fresh basil leaves

1 In 10-inch skillet, heat oil over medium heat. Add onion; cook 10 minutes, stirring occasionally. Reduce heat to medium-low; cook 5 to 10 minutes longer, stirring frequently, until onions are very tender and golden. Remove from heat; set aside.

2 Heat gas or charcoal grill for indirect cooking as directed by manufacturer. Spray large cookie sheet with cooking spray. Unroll can of dough; cut into 4 equal rectangles. Spray both sides of each rectangle with cooking spray; place on cookie sheet.

3 Place 2 dough rectangles at a time directly on grill rack on unheated side of two-burner gas grill or over drip pan on charcoal grill. (If using one-burner gas grill, cook over low heat.) Cover grill; cook 5 to 7 minutes or until edges of dough look dry (check occasionally to make sure bottoms of crusts are cooking evenly; rotate crusts if necessary). Cook about 2 minutes longer or until bottoms of crusts are golden and have grill marks. Using large pancake turner, remove crusts from grill to cookie sheet. Repeat with remaining dough rectangles.

4 Turn cooked crusts over so cooked sides are up; spread evenly with pizza sauce. Top each with sausage, onions and cheese.

5 Return pizzas to grill rack over indirect heat. Cover grill; cook about 5 minutes longer or until bottoms are golden brown and cheese is melted. Sprinkle with basil.

1 Individual Pizza: Calories 500; Total Fat 22g (Saturated Fat 9g, Trans Fat 0g); Cholesterol 40mg; Sodium 1290mg; Total Carbohydrate 55g (Dietary Fiber 3g); Protein 21g **Exchanges:** 1 Starch, 2½ Other Carbohydrate, 2½ High-Fat Meat, ½ Fat **Carbohydrate Choices:** 3½

Tip Any type of precooked sausage can be used instead of kielbasa. Or try pepperoni, Canadian bacon, cooked chorizo or your favorite veggies.

Deep Dish Pizza Pie

Prep Time: 20 Minutes • **Start to Finish:** 1 Hour • Makes 8 servings

1 lb bulk reduced-fat Italian pork sausage

1 large onion, chopped (1 cup)

1 small green bell pepper, chopped

2 cups Original Bisquick mix

½ cup stone-ground yellow cornmeal

½ cup shredded Parmesan cheese (2 oz)

6 tablespoons cold butter

¼ cup boiling water

6 slices (¾ oz each) mozzarella cheese

⅔ cup pizza sauce

1 package (3 oz) sliced pepperoni

2 cups shredded mozzarella cheese (8 oz)

Small fresh basil leaves, if desired

1 Heat oven to 350°F. In 12-inch nonstick skillet, cook sausage over medium heat until no longer pink. Remove sausage to paper towels, reserving drippings. Cook onion and bell pepper in drippings until crisp-tender.

2 In medium bowl, stir Bisquick mix, cornmeal and Parmesan cheese. Cut in butter, using pastry blender or fork, until crumbly. Add boiling water; stir vigorously until dough forms. Spray 10-inch ovenproof skillet with cooking spray. Press dough on bottom and up side of skillet. Arrange cheese slices over crust; spread with ⅓ cup of the pizza sauce. Top with sausage and onion mixture. Arrange two-thirds of the pepperoni over onion mixture. Spread remaining ⅓ cup pizza sauce over pepperoni; top with shredded mozzarella cheese and remaining pepperoni.

3 Bake 30 to 35 minutes or until crust is golden brown. Let stand 5 minutes. Garnish with basil. Serve with additional pizza sauce, heated, if desired.

1 Serving: Calories 585; Total Fat 39g (Saturated Fat 19g, Trans Fat 0g); Cholesterol 0mg; Sodium 506mg; Total Carbohydrate 34g (Dietary Fiber 2g); Protein 30g **Exchanges:** 1½ Starch, ½ Vegetable, 2 Medium-Fat Meat, 2 Fat **Carbohydrate Choices:** 1½

Metric Conversion Guide

Volume

U.S. Units	Canadian Metric	Australian Metric
¼ teaspoon	1 mL	1 ml
½ teaspoon	2 mL	2 ml
1 teaspoon	5 mL	5 ml
1 tablespoon	15 mL	20 ml
¼ cup	50 mL	60 ml
⅓ cup	75 mL	80 ml
½ cup	125 mL	125 ml
⅔ cup	150 mL	170 ml
¾ cup	175 mL	190 ml
1 cup	250 mL	250 ml
1 quart	1 liter	1 liter
1½ quarts	1.5 liters	1.5 liters
2 quarts	2 liters	2 liters
2½ quarts	2.5 liters	2.5 liters
3 quarts	3 liters	3 liters
4 quarts	4 liters	4 liters

Weight

U.S. Units	Canadian Metric	Australian Metric
1 ounce	30 grams	30 grams
2 ounces	55 grams	60 grams
3 ounces	85 grams	90 grams
4 ounces (¼ pound)	115 grams	125 grams
8 ounces (½ pound)	225 grams	225 grams
16 ounces (1 pound)	455 grams	500 grams
1 pound	455 grams	0.5 kilogram

Note: The recipes in this cookbook have not been developed or tested using metric measures. When converting recipes to metric, some variations in quality may be noted.

Measurements

Inches	Centimeters
1	2.5
2	5.0
3	7.5
4	10.0
5	12.5
6	15.0
7	17.5
8	20.5
9	23.0
10	25.5
11	28.0
12	30.5
13	33.0

Temperatures

Fahrenheit	Celsius
32°	0°
212°	100°
250°	120°
275°	140°
300°	150°
325°	160°
350°	180°
375°	190°
400°	200°
425°	220°
450°	230°
475°	240°
500°	260°

Recipe Testing and Calculating Nutrition Information

Recipe Testing:

· Large eggs and 2% milk were used unless otherwise indicated.

· Fat-free, low-fat, low-sodium or lite products were not used unless indicated.

· No nonstick cookware and bakeware were used unless otherwise indicated. No dark-colored, black or insulated bakeware was used.

· When a pan is specified, a metal pan was used; a baking dish or pie plate means ovenproof glass was used.

· An electric hand mixer was used for mixing only when mixer speeds are specified.

Calculating Nutrition:

· The first ingredient was used wherever a choice is given, such as ⅓ cup sour cream or plain yogurt.

· The first amount was used wherever a range is given, such as 3- to 3½-pound whole chicken.

· The first serving number was used wherever a range is given, such 4 to 6 servings.

· "If desired" ingredients were not included.

· Only the amount of a marinade or frying oil that is absorbed was included.

America's most trusted cookbook is better than ever!

- 1,100 all-new photos, including hundreds of step-by-step images
- More than 1,500 recipes, with hundreds of inspiring variations and creative "mini" recipes for easy cooking ideas
- Brand-new features
- Gorgeous new design

Get the best edition of the *Betty Crocker Cookbook* today!

CPSIA information can be obtained
at www.ICGtesting.com
Printed in the USA
BVHW01s0939260818
525620BV00008B/95/P

9 780544 314832